Build a Tree

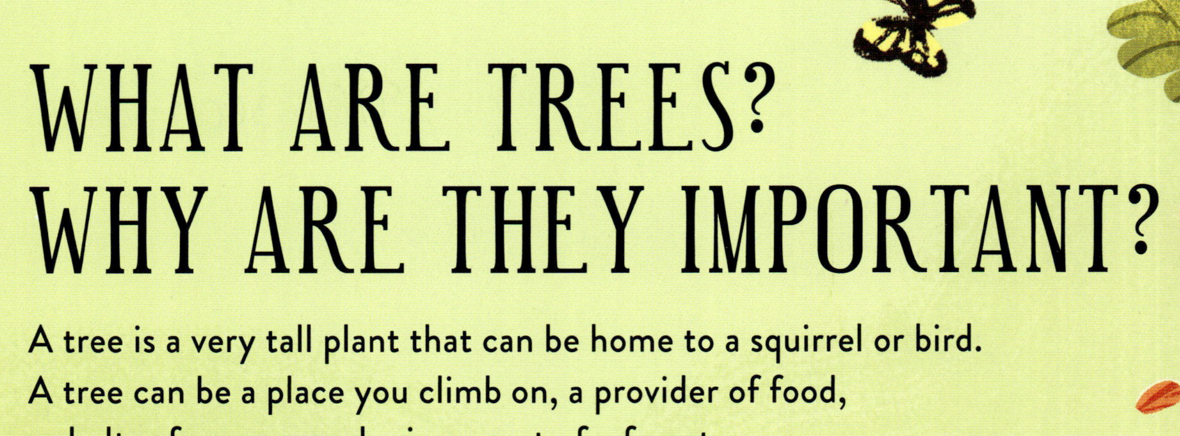

WHAT ARE TREES? WHY ARE THEY IMPORTANT?

A tree is a very tall plant that can be home to a squirrel or bird. A tree can be a place you climb on, a provider of food, a shelter from sun and rain or part of a forest. Trees are all these things and more, but above all they are wonderful and really important for all life on our planet.

TREES ARE HABITATS

Every part of a tree creates habitats. Each leaf, branch, and root system is home to creatures big and small. There are more than 58,000 named tree species worldwide, each home to an amazing variety of other plants and animals.

THE BOTANICAL BIT

A tree is a tall, woody, branched plant. Trees are perennials, which means they grow more every year. Grasses, shrubs and mosses are some other types of plant.

trunk—a long, strong stem that is encased in bark; it supports the branches and transports water, nutrients, and energy from the roots

roots—absorb water and nutrients from the soil

LEAVES HELP TREES GROW

Inside each leaf, light, carbon dioxide from the air, and water are used to make a sugary substance called glucose. This provides the energy that a tree needs for growth.

TREES HELP THE ENVIRONMENT

Carbon dioxide is one of the greenhouse gases responsible for climate change. Trees are vital to reducing the effects of climate change on our planet, because as they grow, they take carbon dioxide from the air and lock it away.

A CARBON SINK

Some of the carbon dioxide from trees enters the woodland soil and is stored there. This means that forests can remove lots of carbon dioxide from our atmosphere, making them amazing 'carbon sinks'.

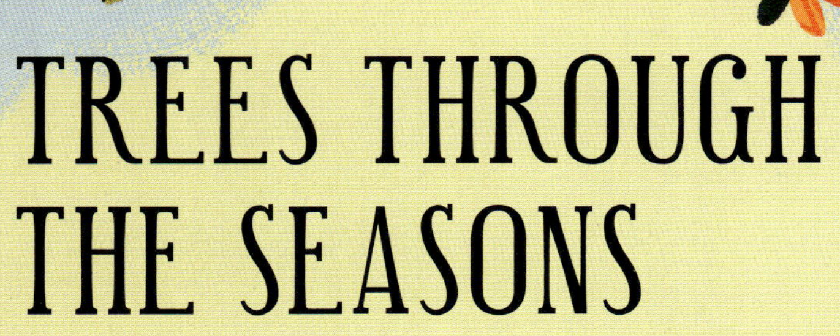

TREES THROUGH THE SEASONS

Trees adapt to changing seasons in different ways. As the amount of daylight varies throughout the year, deciduous trees make big and obvious changes in response. Trees such as oak and beech change their leaf cover all year round and make the most of the seasons to grow and reproduce.

IN SPRING: FLOWERS

In spring, new leaves grow from buds and tree flowers blossom. Some flowers use smell, color, shape, and nectar to attract pollinators such as birds, bees, butterflies, or bats. They fly from flower to flower, exchanging pollen as they go. Trees with catkin-type flowers, such as oaks, use the wind to blow pollen between them. Without pollen, flowers can't create seeds and there would be no flowering trees!

IN SUMMER: FRUIT

Throughout summer, when there is the most daylight and sunshine, leaves make lots of food to help pollinated flowers turn into fruits. The oak grows acorns, the beech produces masts, the hazel makes nuts and the apple tree makes apples. A fruit is how a tree protects its new seeds.

CONIFEROUS TREES

Conifer trees, such as pines or spruces, have leaves shaped like needles. Conifers never lose all their leaves because they often live in colder climates with less daylight. They shed and regrow leaves all year round. Conifers make cones instead of flowers and the wind carries pollen from male to female cones. Here seeds develop, protected under hard overlapping scales. In dry weather, the scales open to release the seeds.

IN AUTUMN: FALLING LEAVES

During autumn, as daylight reduces, tree leaves die, change color and finally fall to the ground. The word deciduous (from the Latin word, *deciduus*), literally means 'falling down'. The now-ripe fruits attract animals, who help to spread tree seeds far and wide.

IN WINTER: FROZEN IN TIME

During the freezing winter months, tree branches are bare. Daylight hours are short so the trees are dormant, saving their energy until spring arrives again.

TYPES OF FOREST

Different trees grow better in different environments and support different kinds of animals, fungi, and plants. This means every region of the world has a different type of forest. Here are four of the most widespread forest types from around the globe.

BOREAL FORESTS

These forests are the most northern. They exist where there are short growing seasons (130 days), low light, and long, cold winters. The soil is poor and shallow. Conifers are the most common kind of tree.

MANGROVE FORESTS

Mangrove trees can't survive the cold, so they live near the equator. They grow in tidal coastal waters. Unlike most trees, they can expel salt from their system to allow them to survive the sea water. Their roots grow out of the ground to allow for the tide changing the water level twice a day. These forests are very biodiverse, providing a vital habitat for young fish and other creatures, and they stabilize the coastline, preventing erosion.

TEMPERATE FORESTS

These forests make up 25 percent of the world's forests and have to cope with warm summers and cold winters. Many trees here drop their leaves in winter and become dormant (the plant version of sleeping) to save energy. Temperate forest trees include oaks, conifers, ash, maple, beech, eucalyptus, olive, and even the giant sequoia trees.

TROPICAL RAINFORESTS

These forests grow in areas with plenty of sunlight, warmth, and rain, and life can flourish here all year round. Although they cover only 10 percent of the Earth's surface, they contain over half the species on the planet, making them precious places for biodiversity. Trees here include kapok, rubber, mahogany, brazil nut, and palm trees.

EXTREME TREES

An adaptation is a special feature that helps a plant or animal survive in a certain place. Trees around the world have evolved some really smart adaptations to live in different conditions, some of which are quite extreme!

IN RAIN OR SHINE

Some types of oak tree can survive long periods without rain because they have adapted to grow deep root systems to find water—including a really long 'tap root.' Deep roots also make the tree more stable in windy conditions.

IN COLD

Conifers, such as pine trees, often live in cold places. Their sloping branches help heavy snow to slip off easily. To stop the trunk freezing, air pockets in the bark act as insulation. Pine needles are thick and waxy to keep water inside, as frozen water in the ground can't be used by the tree. Pines also grow together in dense forests for protection and extra warmth.

IN HEAT

Eucalypts native to Australia have tough, leathery leaves that don't wilt easily. This helps them survive in hot, dry conditions and even deserts. They can also resprout very quickly from dormant buds under the bark to help the tree recover quickly from frequent forest fires.

IN SHALLOW SOIL

The sessile oak tree spreads out its root system in shallow soil to soak up rainwater before it drains away. Many large tropical rainforest trees form buttresses around their base for extra stability. This often happens where the soil is very shallow and roots can't grow far down.

IN FIRE

Sequoia trees and redwoods don't mind fire at all because they are flame resistant! A chemical called tannic acid in their thick bark prevents them from catching fire. If the forest around them does ignite, pine saplings and firs—which have thinner bark—burn up and create a bed of ash. Heated by the fire, the cones of the sequoia trees open and drop their seeds onto the fertile ash, where they grow into new trees.

CANOPY LIFE

High above the ground, the thick forest canopy contains most of the trees' branches, twigs and leaves—the crowns of all the trees. Millions of animal and plant species can be found in the treetops.

DIFFERENT WEATHER?

In the canopy, the conditions can be different from those on the ground, with more sunshine, higher temperatures and more wind. Treetops affect the local climate, too, by shading the earth from the sun and absorbing warmth from the ground. A large forested area can even encourage more rainfall.

NEW SCIENCE

In 1982, insect expert Terry Erwin "fogged" some tropical trees with chemicals. This made all of the trees' insects fall to the ground where he could count them. He estimated that there were twice as many insects in the trees as on the forest floor. Now, scientists think there might be even more than that.

ARBORNAUTS

Arbornauts use new climbing methods to explore the tree canopy. They use ropes and walkways, camera traps, balloons and cranes to study canopy wildlife, it's an exciting new area for science.

EPIPHYTES

Thousands of beautiful orchids, mosses, ferns and bromeliads thrive high in the canopy, providing food for many birds and animals. They are epiphytes (plants which grow on other plants) and use the nutrients in rain and mist to grow.

PARACHUTING FROGS

Some canopy frogs have evolved huge webbed feet, not for swimming but for "flying". To escape predators, they leap and then glide more than 49 feet! Sticky toe pads help them land safely!

HOWLING MONKEYS

Howler monkeys are famous for their booming calls, making them the loudest land animal. Howling is a great way to communicate for miles across the forest canopy. The monkeys can dangle from a branch, supporting their entire weight with their tail. They love eating fruit, and their poop helps to spread fruit tree seeds around the forest.

ON THE FOREST FLOOR

It may seem quiet, but the forest floor is buzzing with activity. All kinds of creatures, from tiny insects to large mammals, live among the dead leaves, fallen fruit, and seeds, which provide them with food and shelter. New discoveries reveal that trees might even be able to communicate with each other through vast underground networks of fungi.

ACORNS

Acorns are large nuts that grow on oak trees. When acorns fall to the ground, squirrels often collect and bury them so they have a store of food for the winter. Sometimes they bury so many they forget where they are. Those acorns aren't wasted. In fact, the forgetful squirrel has helped the tree by planting the acorn, so it can grow into a new oak.

FUEL FOR GROWTH

Dead and decaying matter, like fallen leaves, is broken down by creatures such as worms and fungi. The nutrients are released into the soil and taken up by other plants, becoming fuel for new growth.

AMERICAN ASPEN

The most widespread tree in North America is the aspen, famous for its beautiful autumn colors. Amazingly, each aspen tree is actually just a shoot of a single massive plant—a small part of one giant underground root system. The Pando aspen in Fishlake National Forest, Utah, has over 40,000 trees, spreads over 106 acres and is the heaviest known living thing. It is thought to be between 8,000 and 12,000 years old.

WALKING LEAVES

Not all animals are content to wait for leaves to fall before they eat them! For example, in tropical rainforests, leafcutter ants use their sharp jaws to cut leaves into pieces before carrying them back to their nests, where they use the leaves to grow fungi that they eat.

DEAD LEAVES

When trees lose their leaves in autumn, the leaves fall to the ground, decay, and form leaf mold. This rich food source is great for worms, woodlice, and beetles, as well as fungi. Hedgehogs, snakes, and even amphibians can all find shelter in the leaf piles, and birds flick through them in search of tasty worms.

SECRET MESSAGES

Hidden underground is a vast web of mycelia: threadlike fungus roots. In a forest, this web acts almost like an extension of tree roots, helping supply more water and break down nutrients for the tree. In return the fungus, which cannot make its own food, receives sugars by tapping into the tree roots. Recently, scientists have discovered that trees might be able to communicate with each other using these hidden networks, even sending more water or nutrients to trees in need, or picking up distress signals from trees under attack.

TREES, BIRDS, AND ANIMALS

All over the world, trees are homes and pantries for many. Leaves, flowers, fruit, and seeds provide food, while trunks and branches are places to create homes and nests. Many trees and animals form living partnerships and couldn't survive without each other.

GREY AND RED SQUIRRELS

Squirrels love to feast on tree nuts and seeds. Red squirrels love conifer and deciduous woodlands, and eat hazelnuts and conifer seeds. Grey squirrels are often seen burying acorns as a winter food store.

GALL WASPS IN OAK TREES

If you look closely, you might spot a strange, round bump dangling from an oak tree's branches. When an insect called a gall wasp lands on a bud or leaf, it injects an egg into it. A grub then hatches and feeds on the tree cells around it. The oak responds by making more cells. This creates a solid bubble—called a gall—around its attacker. Eventually, the gall falls from the tree and the grub emerges as an adult wasp.

UNDER THE PINE NEEDLES

The layer of fallen needles in a conifer forest might not look like a very inviting place to live, but it is full of life. Millions of tiny mites thrive here. Some eat the needles, some hunt worms, and some even hunt other mites.

GREEN WOODPECKER

The green woodpecker's head is specially evolved to protect its brain from the drumming of its beak as it makes its nest hole in a tree trunk. Special claws grip onto bark as a retractable tongue, that extends nearly 6 inches, grabs ants or larvae from nooks and crannies.

BEAR SCRATCH POSTS

Bears use trees as scratching posts! They often have a favorite tree to return to. The bears also claw and debark the tree. Some scientists even think that the tree's resin acts as an insect repellent, which helps to keep blood-sucking ticks away.

CECROPIA

This small tropical tree is home to Azteca ants. It is found in clearings where there are few other plants to compete with. If another plant tries to grow nearby, the ants attack by stinging it and injecting poison that kills the new plant. In return, the tree provides a home in its hollow stems and even produces special energy-rich food parcels for the ants to eat.

NATURAL THREATS TO TREES

The world can be an unpredictable place for all living things. Over such long lives, trees will encounter all sorts of natural threats, so some have adaptations to deal with them.

DROUGHT

As our climate changes, long and severe droughts are becoming more common in places such as Kenya and New Mexico in the USA. These extreme droughts change the soil, make trees unhealthy, and dry out forests.

FIRE AND STORMS

Lightning strikes often cause fires in Yellowstone National Park. In 1988, record-breaking fires affected almost 800,000 acres—36 percent of the park. In some places, new growth began within a few days. Today, young trees cover the landscape once more.

Although it is destructive, fire is a natural part of a forest's ecosystem. Fire can even help plants to grow by clearing space in the forest. Some trees have thick bark that doesn't burn easily and protects the inside of the trunk.

DISEASE

Trees are more likely to catch a disease if they aren't healthy. From root rot to canker, blight to rusts, there are many different kinds of tree disease.

Ash dieback

Eighty percent of ash trees in the UK could be lost to this fungus. When a wind-borne spore lands on a leaf, it penetrates the tree and grows, blocking the water and food transportation system until, slowly, the tree dies. Scientists are working hard to find a cure.

PESTS

In some states and in Yellowstone National Park, the white bark pine tree lives on the timberline, a high, cool place where other trees struggle to thrive. Grizzly bears love their energy-rich seeds, which help the bears gain a thick layer of fat for hibernation. Milder winters and warmer temperatures mean the deadly mountain pine bark beetle is spreading. It feeds on the cambium layer of the trunk—the growing part just inside the bark—and kills trees.

Mountain pine bark beetle

WHY DO WE NEED TREES?

Animals and plants rely on trees as habitat and food. For humans, trees not only make the world better but are also essential to our survival on Earth.

TREES REDUCE GLOBAL WARMING

As well as providing us with oxygen, trees lock up carbon dioxide for centuries. Carbon dioxide is a greenhouse gas which contributes to global warming, and we all need to try to reduce it as much as possible.

URBAN TREES

Trees don't just belong in the countryside—in towns and cities they provide shelter and protection from wind. In summer, as water evaporates from their leaves, they have a much needed cooling effect. Trees planted around buildings can help cut the need for air-conditioning by providing shade. They also act as giant filters for the pollution we create. Trees can absorb harmful particles emitted by traffic and factories—making the air we breathe fresh and clean.

TREES PROVIDE US WITH FOOD

Apples, pears, almonds, cherries, chestnuts, and coconuts are just a few of the many foods our trees provide us with. Even the cork we use in our bottles comes from the cork oak tree—so they help us with packaging, too!

TREES ARE GOOD FOR OUR HEALTH

Studies have proven that "forest bathing" or walking in the woods can help us feel less anxious, improve our mood, make us more creative, and improve our health. This happens because trees have special oils (phytoncides) to ward off attacks from bacteria, insects, and fungi, which can also affect humans in positive ways. Not only that, but in a forest there is more oxygen, which boosts our energy levels. It has also been shown that people in hospital beds with a view of trees actually recover from illness faster.

TREES PREVENT FLOODING

Forests and trees act as natural sponges and can play a vital part in preventing floods. As a natural store for rainwater, trees can prevent water from running rapidly off the ground's surface and flooding local areas. Similarly, tree roots hold soil in place on sloping ground, preventing flood waters from washing it away.

HUMAN THREATS TO TREES IN NUMBERS

We need trees and yet human activity continues to chop them down faster than they can naturally regenerate. One third of tree species are threatened with extinction. That's 17,510 species—a tree extinction crisis.

Although 58,000 tree species have been recorded, the most recent estimate is that there are around 73,000 plus at least 9,000 still unknown.

142 tree species are recorded as Extinct or Extinct in the Wild.

Roughly **40 percent** of undiscovered tree species are in South America. The most threatened trees grow in the tropics.

Around **15.3 billion** trees are destroyed by human activity each year in the following ways:

29%

AGRICULTURE 29%

Forest clearing for farming is the biggest threat to trees worldwide. This land is mainly used to produce coffee, soybeans, and palm oil.

27%

LOGGING 27%

Humans have chopped down trees all over the world for hundreds of years, but demand has grown higher and faster over the last 200 years. By the 19th century, only 5 percent of land in Great Britain remained as forest. Now, only a handful of large deciduous forests are left in Europe.

In the USA, San Francisco was originally built with the wood from the 2 million acres of redwood forests that ran for 500 miles along the Pacific Northwest.

CLIMATE CHANGE 4%
Climate change causes all sorts of extra challenges for trees, such as drought and even extinction.
INVASIVE SPECIES AND PESTS 5%
The changing climate, an increase in international trade and travel, and the introduction of non-native species have all affected our trees.
WOOD AND PULP PLANTATION 6%
Unsustainable production of wood pulp to make paper, tissue, and packaging has a devastating effect on forests.
FIRE 13%
In some places, fire is a natural part of forest life. But in the tropics, where rainforests rarely burn naturally, some are deliberately set on fire to clear space for roads, cattle, and crops. In 2022 alone, over **19.5 million acres** of Brazil's Amazon rainforest was burned.
4%
5%
6%
13%
13%
DEVELOPMENT 13%
Towns, villages, roads, and railways all take land from trees.

CONSERVING OUR TREES

Trees are so important to life on Earth that we should all feel responsible for them. We can all help to keep them safe, and there are many tree heroes to be inspired by.

Wangarĩ Maathai

After becoming the first woman in East and Central Africa to earn her doctorate degree, Wangarĩ introduced community-based tree planting, helping to reduce poverty and help the environment. She founded the Green Belt Movement in 1977 and won the Nobel Peace Prize in 2004.

John Muir is known as an advocate of USA forest conservation. He was responsible for taking President Roosevelt on the camping trip into what is now Yosemite National Park which inspired the President to protect the redwoods. Muir also headed the campaign to create Yosemite National Park.

The City of Paris

In France, Paris has a newly planted urban forest of trees. Since 2020, thousands of trees have been planted, with an estimated 170,000 trees to be planted in total. It is hoped the trees will help cool the city, and some of them even have probes to measure water stress and make sure they get enough water.

Julia Butterfly Hill is the girl who lived for 2 years (1997–99), 200 feet above the ground in a 1,000-year-old redwood tree to prevent the Pacific Lumber Company from cutting it down. She saved the tree and raised awareness on TV.

HOW CAN WE HELP?

We can all play our part in saving the world's trees. We can:

- encourage decision-makers, such as politicians, to take action to protect tree biodiversity and support charities including WWF and the International Tree Foundation, who are already taking action.
- buy wood and paper products from sustainable sources.
- reduce the number of products we buy that are destroying natural forests. For example, products containing some sources of soya, palm oil, and tropical hardwoods.
- support local tree planting organizations that protect our natural forests. Choose those that plant native and threatened species.
- plant more trees. If you find an acorn on the ground, perhaps you could plant it and care for it so it grows into a beautiful oak tree.

FAMOUS TREES

Some trees are so special that they have become famous, surviving for centuries and earning a place in our hearts and history books. Here are just a few of them, but now that you know how special trees really are, you may want to discover and protect more yourself.

LARGEST

General Sherman, a sequoia in Sequoia National Park in California, USA, is the largest tree in the world and the largest living thing. It was named after William T. Sherman, a commander in the American Civil War.

OLDEST

Methuselah, a bristlecone pine in the White Mountains of California, USA, was discovered by Dr. Edmund Schulman in the 1950s. At least 4,600 years old, it is thought to be the oldest living tree known to science.

MOST WORSHIPPED

In New Zealand, **kauri** trees are considered sacred by the Māori people. From around 200 years ago, English settlers chopped them down until there were just a few left. One, *Te Matua Ngahere* (Father of the Forest), is still watched over by Māori guardians.

The chapel oak (Allouville-Bellefosse, Normandy, France)

In 1696, a chapel was built inside this huge hollow oak. When the top was blown off by lightning the local people built a tower on it, and when the bark peeled off they covered it in shingles. The chapel looks like something from a fairy tale and is still used today.

Sacred **camphor trees** grow in the Shinto shrines of Japan and are decorated with ropes, tassels, and paper lanterns. People pray to the tree's spirit and believe that each time they circle it, a year is added to their life.

HISTORIC TREES

The Great Plane Tree of Hippocrates

Legend says that this was the tree under which Hippocrates, the father of medicine, taught in the 5th century BCE. These days its trunk is protected by a metal cage.

GLOSSARY

ADAPT to change in order to be better suited to conditions in an environment

ARBORNAUT a researcher or explorer who studies the treetops of forests

BIODIVERSE having many different types of living things

BLIGHT a plant disease usually caused by fungi

BUTTRESS a type of root that grows out from the tree trunk to help to support the tree

CANKER a tree disease caused by a fungus that damages the tree's bark

CANOPY the branches and leaves at the very top of a group of trees

CARBON a chemical element that is found in all living things and is essential for life

CARBON DIOXIDE the gas formed when carbon is burned, or when people or animals breathe out

CHLOROPHYLL the green substance in green plants that allows them to use the energy from the Sun

CLIMATE CHANGE changes in Earth's weather caused by the increase of carbon dioxide in the atmosphere due to human activity

CONIFEROUS a type of tree that produces cones and has needles for leaves that don't fall in winter

DECAY to slowly rot and break down

DECIDUOUS a type of tree that loses its leaves in autumn and grows new ones in spring

DORMANT alive but not growing

DROUGHT a long, dry period when there is little to no rainfall

ECOSYSTEM all the living things in an area interacting with each other and all the non-living things such as water, soil, and weather

EROSION the wearing away of rocks and soil by natural forces such as water, wind, or ice

FERTILE describes a land or soil that produces lots of crops

FUNGUS a type of living thing that is neither plant nor animal, such as a mushroom or mold

GLUCOSE a type of sugar found in plants that is an important supply of energy for animals

GREENHOUSE GAS one of the gases in Earth's atmosphere that trap heat and are essential for life. Human activity has increased levels of some of these gases, such as carbon dioxide, causing Earth to heat up too much.

GRUB an insect in the stage just after it has come out of the egg, usually soft and wormlike

NECTAR a sweet liquid produced by flowers that is collected by bees and other insects

NUTRIENT a substance that living things need to live and grow

OXYGEN a gas that is needed by all living things to survive. Plants produce it.

PHOTOSYNTHESIS the process in which a plant uses carbon dioxide from the air, water from the ground, and sunlight to produce its own food and oxygen

POLLINATOR usually an insect that carries pollen from plant to plant

PROBE an instrument that is put inside something to test or record information

RUST a plant disease that causes reddish-brown spots

SHINGLE a rectangular tile used to cover walls or roofs

SPORE a reproductive cell produced by some living things, such as ferns and mushrooms

STOMATA very small holes in the surface of a leaf or stem of a plant through which gases are able to pass in and out

SUSTAINABLE causing, or made in a way that causes, little or no damage to the environment and therefore able to continue for a long time

BUILD THE TREE

Assemble the tree by slotting the numbered pieces together as shown in the diagrams.

BUILDING TIP:
Press out the pieces as you need them so you don't lose track of the numbers.

STEP ONE: THE TRUNK
Slot parts A1 and A2 together to form the trunk. Slide part A3 onto the top of the trunk, lining up the corresponding slots with A1 and A2.

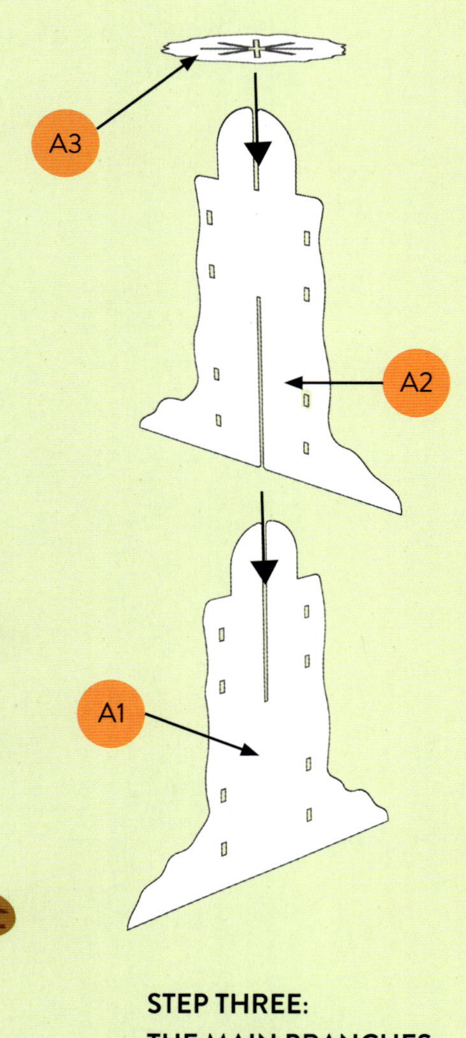

STEP TWO: STRENGTHENING THE TRUNK
Clip all four parts of C into the trunk (A1 and A2) by lining up the slots and pushing them into the slits.

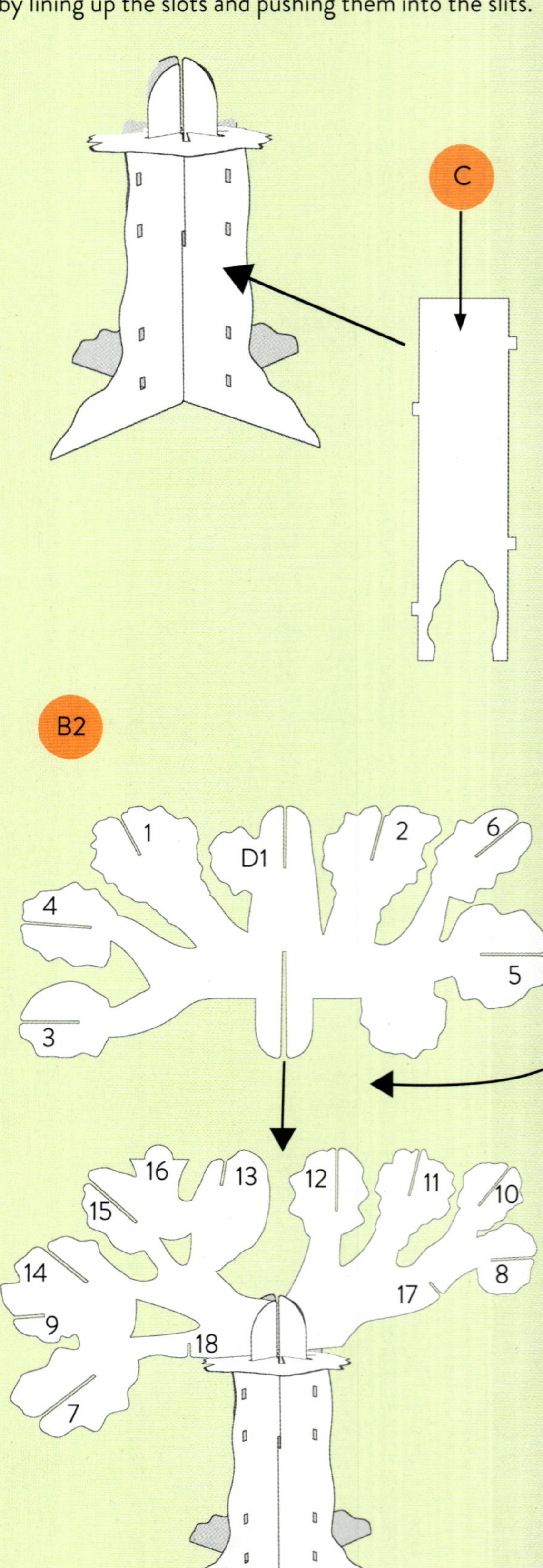

STEP THREE:
THE MAIN BRANCHES
Slide B1 into A3. Then slide B2 over B1 and into A3, making sure to link up the matching colors so that each quarter of the tree depicts a different season.